Your Cat's Astrological Horoscope

Images taken from KozmoPets™ series by L. Matusovsky

"I speak to thee in silence."

                    –Shakespeare

Contents

About the book

Your Cat's Lifetime horoscope is one of the few publications of its kind to explain the use of astrology in understanding the lives and fates of animals. You'll find new ways to relate to your pet as you unlock the door to your cat's real astro personality and develop perfect harmony with your treasured feline friend. This innovative work provides you with a sun-sign map to your cat's motivations and desires. You'll find useful information for choosing the best mate for your cat, for selecting a pet who will live in astrological harmony with other household pets, for picking the right name according to your kitten's Zodiac sign – even for determining the best time to walk your cat. Your Cat's Lifetime Horoscope provides new information and insight for every cat lover who wants to achieve greater communication with these ideal companions.

This is a 'must have' book for you and your best friend. Everything found in Your Cat's Lifetime Horoscope – based on the best astrological practices – is designed to reveal the inner life and true cat personality to both new and long-time pet lovers. With this book, you can use your pet's sun-sign to:

- Find the perfect match for you and your lifestyle using the highly detailed astrological information inside.
- Choose the best name for your pet with a never-before seen astrological formula.
- Document the arrival – make your cat an official member of your family with a never-before seen Zodiac Birth Certificate.

Introduction

This book explains how astrology works in the lives of animals. If you are a cat lover, you probably want to learn all you can about cat behavior and cats' relationships with humans. This work answers many of your questions while elucidating the undercurrents of cats' instinctive behavior.

Just as people's horoscopes are cast regardless of race or nationality, we do not consider breed when casting cats' horoscopes. Rather, we are concerned with the astral influence of your cat's sun sign. As noted, if you do not know when your cat was born, you should consider the time of his or her appearance in your home the birth month. For your pet, this time is truly the second birth.

I describe the compatibility between the signs of the Zodiac to help you choose the best cat for you. This tool also serves as an excellent guide for cat breeders!

If you have a cat at home, you are already a happy person. If you have problems with your pet, just open our horoscope, find the sun sign, and you'll be on your way to making those problems vanish. Don't have a cat yet? This astrological guide will help you make the perfect choice.

Luba Matusovsky

Aquarius Cat

January 21-February 19

Symbol: The Water Carrier. Aquarius – an Air Sign – belongs to the element which links all living beings – the life force that flows from the atmosphere through our bodies, and out into the atmosphere again.
Key Words: *Friendship, Eccentricity, Freedom.*
Dominant Principle: *"I know"*
Ruling Planet: *Saturn*
Stones: *Light Sapphire, Opal, Amethyst, Garnet*
Metal: *Tin*
Lucky Days: *Wednesday, Saturday*
Unlucky Day: *Sunday*

Aquarian cat is loving but not possessive

Are you the kind of animal lover who takes in every stray you find – even when the house is so crowded there's no room for you? Then I'd better introduce you to Aquarius Cat! You see, Aquarius is the most friendly feline around. Because Aquarius is ruled by two planets, Saturn and Uranus, he is loving but not possessive. He does not have a jealous bone in his body! While some cats would be furious at the sight of a stranger hanging around, hungrily eyeing their dinner, Aquarius Cat likes to play host, sharing his food without so much as a murmur. The amazing thing is that he doesn't even mind sharing you!

An independent fellow, your animal Aquarius will enjoy being both inside and outdoors. He wants to be wherever the action is – so when you're hanging those clothes out to dry, don't be surprised if you suddenly find yourself the sole object of Aquarius Cat's attention. Aquarius is both naturally curious and very theatrical. If he is not hanging from the line like a clothes pin, he will probably be racing off with your underwear!

Well suited to life in a large family where children and pets live in happy, sun-dappled chaos, Aquarius Cat's philosophy is simply, "The more, the merrier!" – except when it comes to food. Like all Air Signs, Aquarius eats lightly but adventurously. Serve your Aquarius hard-to-find delicacies such as minced crab or elegant poached salmon. He will be in heaven!

Because Aquarius Cat is so outgoing, it can be difficult for him to connect with only one owner. It is not unusual for him to form bonds with several members of the household. He may seem fickle at times, but it's merely his way of telling you that he is not a clinger – and you are not allowed to be, either!

Compatibility with other signs:

Harmony: Gemini, Libra
Friendship: Aries, Sagittarius
Conflict: Taurus, Leo, Scorpio
Health Tips: Aquarius may have problems with his blood circulation and heart. He can't handle extreme heat, so when the outside temperature soars, turn on the air conditioning!
What does Aquarius Cat bring you? From the moment he appears in your house, Aquarius Cat compensates for any lack of friendship and security in your life.. He may become a very loyal friend, accompanying you on trips like a devoted dog. He could even protect you against attacks. If Aquarius Cat has found you when the sun is in Aquarius, he is almost certainly a gift from someone in the spirit world. In giving you this special cat, the sender is telling you that you are loved, missed, and remembered.

Pisces Cat

February 20-March 20

Symbol: *Two fish joined together but pulling in opposite directions, embodying Pisces' dual and vacillating nature.*
Key Words: *Sensitive, Indecisive, Compassionate.*
Dominant Principle: *"I believe"*
Ruling Planet: *Jupiter*
Stones: *Sapphire, Moonstone*
Metal: *Zinc*
Lucky days: *Monday, Thursday, Friday*
Unlucky Day: *Wednesday*

The *gentle presence* of your Piscean cat will have you *feeling relaxed*

Deeply sensitive and intuitive, Pisces Cat is a walking, meowing comfort zone! Reeling from a break up with the only person you ever loved? Don't worry, your Pisces pussycat will see you through the pain. Nervous and tense after a tough day at the office? The gentle presence of Pisces Cat will soon have you feeling relaxed. Indeed, Pisces is the most sympathetic and soothing feline in the Zodiac. She is also in a little dream world of her own! Her bright, imaginative mind is like a theater where cat toys such as rubber mice and bouncy, multi-colored balls play starring roles. Shower her with as many toys as you like! She'll truly appreciate them.

Best suited for quiet households (her natural love of the ethereal doesn't gel with chaos), Pisces Cat usually finds the outside world alarming and confusing. Everyday noises – traffic, airplanes – sound like thunder to your furry little Pisces. She'll be happiest if you keep her indoors.

In keeping with Pisces' gentle nature, don't lunge at your cat hoping to smother her in a bear hug. As sweet and loyal as your Pisces kitty is, she hates to feel constricted. Give her lots of physical space and make sure she has a loose-fitting fabric (not leather) collar.

Pisces Cat likes to eat anything moist – she's a Water Sign, after all! Try mixing some liquid (the runoff from a can of tuna is nice!) in with her crunchy food. Having salmon mousse for dinner? Don't forget to treat your Pisces pet to the leftovers, because they're exactly what she craves. Whip her up a serving of white fish, cream her up some crab, even purée her a little lobster, and you'll have the most contented feline on Earth – when she comes back down to it!

Compatibility with other signs:

Harmony: Cancer, Scorpio
Friendship: Taurus, Capricorn
Conflict: Gemini, Virgo, Sagittarius
Health Tips: Pisces Cat may experience problems in her abdominal region. Also, she will do better in a dry climate; damp weather may have an adverse effect.

What does Pisces Cat bring you? If you get a Pisces Cat (or any cat during the Pisces period) it indicates Karmic ties. You have been destined to meet! She came to share your solitary existence and heal your wounds with her love.

Aries Cat

March 21-April 20

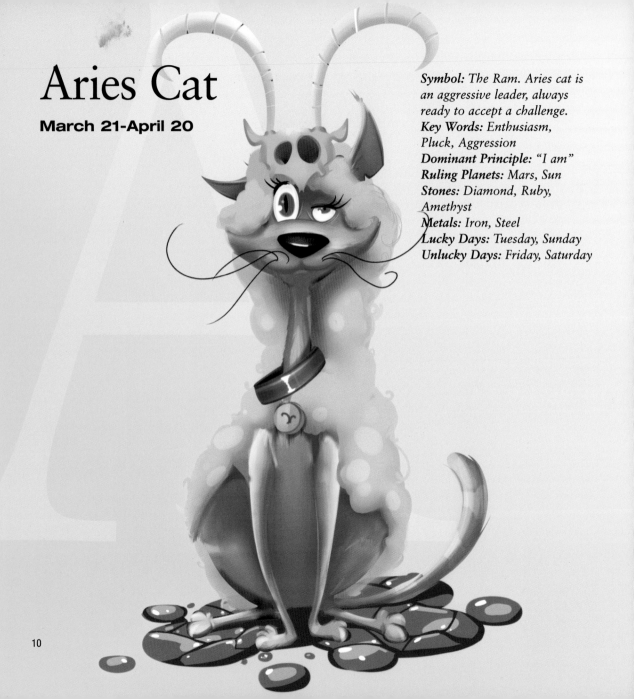

Symbol: *The Ram. Aries cat is an aggressive leader, always ready to accept a challenge.*
Key Words: *Enthusiasm, Pluck, Aggression*
Dominant Principle: *"I am"*
Ruling Planets: *Mars, Sun*
Stones: *Diamond, Ruby, Amethyst*
Metals: *Iron, Steel*
Lucky Days: *Tuesday, Sunday*
Unlucky Days: *Friday, Saturday*

Arian cats are stubborn, energetic, and full of fight and spirit

As the first sign of the zodiac, Aries begins a new cycle of activity. Aries people have a lot of creative energy, are very aggressive, and often take on leadership roles. But what about Aries cats? They are very similar to their human counterparts: stubborn, energetic, and full of spirit. Their courage makes them natural leaders, in or out of the home. If you have other cats in your household, make sure your aggressive Aries kitty isn't standing guard over the food bowl! The others will hardly be able to get a bite.

Immensely physical and energetic, Aries Cat is the most likely to get herself trapped high in a tree – until the firemen come to rescue her! Don't be surprised if your neighbors are constantly calling to complain about your cat's out-of-control behavior. Disciplining Aries cats can be difficult, as they rarely stand still long enough to listen.

Aries Cat is the ultimate outdoor adventurer: don't get one unless you plan to let him or her roam the outdoors. Confining the cat to the house will only make her miserable. Aries needs an outlet for her energy, so if you must keep your Aries Cat indoors and you like your furniture, make sure you have plenty of scratching posts for her! Remember, an Aries cat is a natural explorer, so give your cat as much freedom as possible.

Although she is fiercely independent, Aries cat does enjoy affection – but only on her own terms. Your cat will let you know when she is ready to be petted. Don't expect to get away with gentle (she might call it lazy) stroking. An Aries cat likes rough love, so give all her itchy spots a thorough scratch.

Compatibility with other signs:

Harmony: Leo, Sagittarius
Friendship: Gemini, Aquarius
Conflict: Cancer, Libra, Capricorn
Health Tips: Aries is highly accident prone, with a tendency for head injuries.
What does Aries Cat bring you? Aries Cat marks a new cycle in your life. Her arrival signals a time of change and new beginnings.

Taurus Cat

April 21-May 21

Symbol: The Bull. Like his symbol – a powerfully built, possessive animal – Taurus is unflinching in attack.
Key Words: Practicality, Possessiveness, Hedonism
Dominant Principle: "I have"
Ruling Planets: Venus, Moon
Stones: Sapphire, Agate, Turquoise, Nephrite
Metal: Copper
Lucky Days: Monday, Friday
Unlucky Day: Tuesday

Taurean cat is a lucky fellow, and he will pass his good luck onto you

As with their human counterparts, Taurus cats love luxury, stability, and good food. The perfect indoor cat, your Taurus is quite happy with a pillow, a shaft of sunlight, and a nice bowl full of kitty crunchies.

Taurus cats demand constant attention and hate to be ignored. They are best suited to owners who work at home – especially since Taureans are often very possessive.

Your Taurus Cat will know if you are planning to sneak off. In fact, he'll probably stand at the door meowing long after you're gone. If you can, leave the lights on or a radio playing whenever you go away. This demonstrates to your insecure Taurus that you are coming back. If you are going away on vacation, try to leave your Taurus Cat with a pet sitter in your own home. The Taurus feline wastes no love on strangers, but would rather be fed by someone he doesn't know than be farmed out to a pet hotel.

Speaking of feeding, your Taurus Cat expects dinner to be served right on the dot. He shuns cheap food – or anything that doesn't come straight off a vet's recommendation list – so don't be surprised if you suddenly find yourself buying one of those cooking-for-kitty books – and sticking to the recipes!

Despite his quirks, you'll find your Taurus Cat undyingly loyal. This is a cat that grows deeply attached to his owner and becomes very emotionally dependent, so if you have other cats this one will probably be a little jealous. Above all, never give away your Taurus Cat unless absolutely necessary, and never, never abandon him. You'll do him no end of harm if you trample his loyal heart by handing him over to someone else.

Taurus Cat is not particularly playful, preferring a comfy couch to the bustling household filled with other pets. Although not an overly sharing and caring kind of kitty, Taurus, with a courteous respect for others' property, is the cat least likely to ruin your furniture or snag your sweater while playing. Taurus Cat is lazy but truly a joy to live with.

Compatibility with other signs:

Harmony: Virgo, Capricorn
Friendship: Cancer, Pisces
Conflict: Leo, Scorpio, Aquarius
Health Tips: Taurus Cat is usually healthy and can live a long life. However, he is susceptible to being overweight, and to having ear and throat infections.
What does Taurus Cat bring you? This cat possesses a golden paw. When he comes into your life, financial improvements are just around the corner; if you are in a difficult phase of your life, Taurus Cat will prove a huge emotional support.

Gemini Cat

May 22-June 21

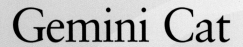

Symbol: The Twins. Gemini's dual nature is reflected in its symbol, which resembles the Roman Numeral II. Gemini Cat may display two very distinct personalities.
Key Words: Inventive, Studious, Active, Sly
Dominant Principle: "I think"
Ruling Planet: Mercury
Stones: Agate, Crystal, Garnet
Metals: Gold, Silver
Lucky Days: Wednesday, Sunday
Unlucky Day: Thursday

Gemini cat *will never* bore you!

While her dual personality will keep you guessing all the time, you can be sure of two things: your Gemini kitty will be both devastatingly overactive and devastatingly charming. One minute she'll be the most delightful, adorable cat on earth; the next she'll be standing on your head, digging in her claws! What you will need is patience – and lots of it! Gemini Cat will get into more scrapes than you imagined possible.

Governed by changeable Mercury, Gemini Cat will never bore you. Your Gemini will have kitty mood swings – up one minute, and even more up the next! Hyper is the word for this cat. Make sure you buy her the very latest in stimulating, high-tech cat toys, but go easy on the catnip. Otherwise your Gemini Cat will leave your house in shambles! In fact, it's best to let Gemini Cat roam the outdoors. Because of her unbridled energy, constant need for stimulation, and strong desire to get into

everything, she'll be easily bored indoors. Outside she'll find trees to climb, neighbors to annoy, and other animals to interact with.

Despite her restlessness, your Gemini Cat is extremely friendly – when she is in the mood.

If you have a good sense of humor and enjoy lots of play, then Gemini is the cat for you. There's nothing she'll appreciate more than hours of rough-housing – especially if she gets to play the star with you as her admiring audience.

Her love of change makes Gemini good at interacting with any other pets you may have. Gemini Cat thrives in a busy household. The constant action keeps her entertained.

As for food, don't even think about feeding her the same thing twice – at least not in one day! A Gemini Cat loves variety, so it's Fancy Feast for one feeding and Nine Lives the next.

Compatibility with other signs:

Harmony: Libra, Aquarius
Friendship: Leo, Aries
Conflict: Sagittarius, Virgo, Pisces
Health Tips: Gemini Cat is prone to exhaustion, circulatory and pulmonary disorders.
What does Gemini Cat bring you? Gemini's greatest gift is protection. She always senses – and warns you of – approaching trouble.

Cancer Cat

June 22-July 23

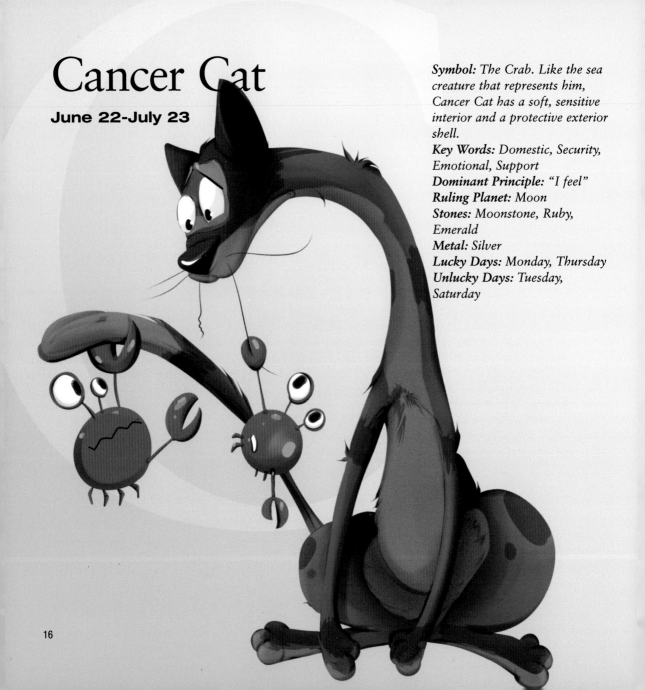

Symbol: The Crab. Like the sea creature that represents him, Cancer Cat has a soft, sensitive interior and a protective exterior shell.
Key Words: Domestic, Security, Emotional, Support
Dominant Principle: "I feel"
Ruling Planet: Moon
Stones: Moonstone, Ruby, Emerald
Metal: Silver
Lucky Days: Monday, Thursday
Unlucky Days: Tuesday, Saturday

Your sensitive Cancer cat
will be the first to comfort you

As Cancer is ruled by the moon, you won't need to dial any of those 1-900 psychic lines with Cancer Cat around – you'll have your very own psychic in the house! Witches are said to have favored Cancer cats as pets, recognizing their unbelievable ability to sense the unknown. But you don't have to be a witch to appreciate Cancer's intuitive skills. Feeling sad? Close to tears? Your sensitive kitty will be the first to comfort you. As he settles in your lap, his eyes will look at you as if to say, "Don't worry. I understand." Or, you may come home to find Cancer Cat waiting at the door for you, just as if he knew you were going to walk in at that very moment. If you live alone or get nervous late at night, Cancer Cat is a good match for you because he'll always sense intruders.

Cancer Cat doesn't appreciate the great outdoors. Instead he prefers the security of a comfy house. If you do have to send your Cancer kitty out into the open, try to offer him the sunny safety of a small garden. Don't worry about the roses. Cancer has a healthy respect for others' property and an uncanny reverence for beauty.

Feeding time for Cancer Cat? Put on your apron! A kitty born under this sign loves smooth and creamy foods, so if you don't have the time to whip up a liver and cream concoction in the blender, make sure you buy a brand of food that goes down easily. The most delicate and expensive of pâtés, along with chicken, veal, and fish are Cancer's favorites, so save the steak for the dog. Milk, associated with mother and security, soothes Cancer Cat's soul, but don't forget that he is a Water Sign. Give him lots of bowls of cool, fresh Evian!

The most important thing to remember about your Cancer cat is that she simply cannot live without affection. Make him (or her) purr long and loud with gentle, loving cuddles.

Compatibility with other signs:

Harmony: Scorpio, Pisces
Friendship: Virgo, Taurus
Conflict: Capricorn, Aries, Libra
Health Tips: Cancer cat has a tendency to be overweight and may acquire diabetes. She may also suffer from kidney disease. What will Cancer Cat bring you? Cancer Cat offers you two great gifts: security and protection.

Leo Cat

July 24-August 23

Symbol: *The Lion. Leo Cat, with his power, his roar, and his regal attitude, takes his cues from the King of the Beasts.*
Key Words: *Power, Generosity, Charisma*
Dominant Principle: *"I will"*
Ruling Planet: *Sun*
Stones: *Amber, Topaz, Emerald, Ruby, Onyx*
Metal: *Gold*
Lucky Day: *Sunday*
Unlucky Day: *Saturday*

Leo kitty wants a comfortable home, *which he alone will rule*

Ruled by the sun, Leo Cat radiates warmth. He also expects to shine. If you are a natural caretaker who enjoys pleasing others, Leo is the perfect cat for you. There's nothing your Leo Cat will appreciate more than being catered to!

Be prepared to have one insulted kitty on your hands if you shove Leo Cat – a handsome and regal specimen – out into the yard! What your Leo kitty really wants is to bask in the glory of a luxuriously comfortable home, which he alone will rule. Although generally courteous and easy-going with other pets, Leo Cat morphs into a lion if someone rudely snatches away his favorite toy. When you go to the pet shop, don't leave without an impressive collection of kitty gadgets that Leo kitty won't have to share – unless he wants to.

Leo can be unfailingly generous, but only on his own terms. Don't forget: gifts go both ways. Don't even think about buying him some scrappy collar from the supermarket, because it simply won't do. It's rhinestones and gold for this kitty, who'll love a showy neckpiece that dangles name tags and bells.

Fire Signs are the Zodiac's meat-eaters, so your Leo Cat will love chunky morsels of expensive, juicy beef and sizable helpings of tender chicken and lamb. Throwing away the remains of that roast you had for dinner? Not so fast. There's a Leo Cat in the household, and if you don't want your garbage turned upside down you'd better serve it to him – preferably on a banquet-sized silver dish. If you are thinking of haunting the aisles for sales on cat food, forget it! Leo Cat will eat only the very finest food you can find.

Although you are probably immersed in your own busy and productive world, Leo Cat couldn't care less! Leo is a demanding guy who expects to always come first. So put down the phone, close your book, and make sure you give him all the attention he wants. Pet him and talk to him constantly. He'll understand every word you say and come back for more!

Compatibility with other signs:

Harmony: Sagittarius, Aries
Friendship: Libra, Gemini
Conflict: Scorpio, Aquarius, Taurus
Health Tips: Leo Cat is generally very healthy, but try not to let him get overweight, because his danger zone is the heart.
What does Leo Cat bring you? Leo Cat's presence reminds you to have confidence in yourself. Walk upright, with your head high, especially when the world has been giving you a hard time.

Virgo Cat

August 24-September 23

Symbol: The Virgin. The only feminine figure in the Zodiac, the Virgin holds an ear of wheat, which symbolizes fertility. She was worshiped as the Earth goddess throughout the ancient world.

Key Words: Service, Practicality, Loyalty

Dominant Principle: "I analyze"

Ruling Planet: Mercury

Stones: Agate, Malachite, Carnelian, Topaz, Nephrite, Yellow Sapphire

Metals: Copper, Tin

Lucky Day: Wednesday

Unlucky Days: Thursday, Friday

Virgo Cat is *compassionate* and loving to the max....

Do you unwind after a long day with a little light housecleaning? Do dirty dishes give you a twitchy eye? If the answer is yes, Virgo is the cat for you. Virgos are extremely fastidious. They love order and schedules. This is why they pace around and around food bowls and litter boxes until someone – namely you – makes sure all is spotless. Virgos are also secretly vain and very into primping. Giving him (or her) a kitty bath might just be Virgo's favorite pastime. (In fact, Virgo can go a little overboard with this.)

Virgos are not your stereotypical lazy cats. While some cats may lay basking in the sun for hours, indolent as ever – and loving it – your Virgo Cat will probably be up and inspecting his surroundings. A stickler for detail, he gives everything the white glove test. Did you change the sheets? Surely you don't expect Virgo Cat to lie on yesterday's scents! If you're not exactly a fanatic about your own sheets, try running Virgo's kitty-bed blankets through the washing machine once in a while. It will make him a much nicer roommate.

All of the above points to one conclusion: Virgo Cat isn't much for the outdoors. In fact, he's somewhat bored by it. Virgo would much rather be inside, overseeing the household. Although he's a natural fusspot, he's got the calm, cool, and collected exterior of a head butler. (Call him Jeeves, if you like!) Virgo Cat is best suited to a quiet household. Chaos and confusion will only make him miserable. Virgo is the perfect companion for a loving senior citizen who might enjoy a devoted – and tidy – pet.

Visitors to the house will love a Virgo kitty because he is usually extremely good-looking. In particular, Virgos tend to have very striking eyes.

Astonishingly sensitive to illness, the Virgo Cat will sometimes lay right on the spot where it hurts, comforting a pain-ridden owner as no one else can.

Compatibility with other signs:

Harmony: Capricorn, Taurus
Friendship: Scorpio, Cancer
Conflict: Sagittarius, Pisces, Gemini
Health Tips: Virgo Cat may be prone to upper respiratory tract infections, which may cause a lack of energy in comparison to other cats. They may also be prone to diabetes and thyroid disease, so ensure that your Virgo Cat follows a healthy diet and gets sufficient exercise.
What does Virgo Cat bring you? Compassionate and loving to the max. Virgo Cat offers oodles and oodles of relief to anyone in discomfort.

Libra Cat

September 24-October 23

Symbol: *The Scales. Libra's symbol is the only inanimate object among the Zodiac signs. Libras seek in others the balancing qualities they lack in themselves. This results in their frequent indecisiveness.*
Key Words: *Cooperation, Companionship, Balance*
Dominant Principle: *"I balance"*
Ruling Planet: *Venus*
Stones: *Opal, Lazurite, Pearl, Chrysolite, Diamond*
Lucky Days: *Friday, Saturday*
Unlucky Days: *Tuesday, Sunday.*

Libran cat can restore broken *harmony in the family*

Libra Cat is an extraordinarily social animal who thrives in the presence of other household pets. In fact, Libra needs to be deeply immersed in a relationship at all times. The Libran scales, ruled by Venus, dictate that any kind of discord sends your Libra kitty scurrying for cover. If you and your spouse or partner are given to constant and lively debate, Libra is not the right feline friend for you. Libra is much happier in a harmonious household where gentle talk is the norm and sunny spots abound.

Libra Cat needs sunlight just as the rest of us need air. He balances this with his need for peace and quiet by enjoying some time indoors and then heading out into the open. Once outside, Libra Cat is not the neighborhood terror. Far from it! You will probably find him dozing in a sunlit corner, indulging his lazy side. When you find him like this, rub his tummy and murmur sweet nothings in his ear! He'll eat it up and ask for more. But don't expect Libra to leap up just because you waved around that cat wand. It is simply not his, or her, style.

While not a fussy eater, don't even think about serving a Libra Cat the same dish twice. Libra Cat craves variety, but also prefers light foods. Make it delicate tuna one day and turkey or chicken the next.

The most important thing to remember about your Libra Cat is that he (or she) loves people. If you have to go away for a few days, try to find an in-house cat-sitter to keep him company. Otherwise your feline friend might get depressed and wander away.

Compatibility with other signs:

Harmony: Aquarius, Gemini
Friendship: Sagittarius Leo
Conflict: Capricorn, Aries, Cancer
Health Tips: Libra Cat is vulnerable to kidney disease. He may also be prone to eye infections.
What does Libra Cat bring you? Because Libra Cat often supplies the emotional support we lack in our human relationships, this cat may arrive in your house when those relationships are suffering. Libra can restore broken harmony in the family and even at work. Try sharing pictures of your kitty companion with coworkers. He may provide the common ground you need to get back on the right track. If you appreciate his dedication, Libra is a very loyal friend.

Scorpio Cat

October 24-November 22

Symbol: *The Scorpion and the Eagle. Together they rise above temptation. This sign is associated with both the life force and the life cycle.*
Key words: *Tenacity, Rebirth, Mystery*
Dominant Principle: *"I desire"*
Ruling Planets: *Pluto, Mars*
Stones: *Ruby, Topaz, Aquamarine, Coral, Malachite*
Metals: *Iron, Steel*
Lucky Day: *Tuesday*
Unlucky Days: *Monday, Friday*

24

You don't *exactly* cuddle up with Scorpio cat....

Scorpio is a natural born leader – and Scorpio Cat insists on taking her rightful place in the household. Often aggressive and powerfully built, Scorpio may intimidate other pets. Don't be surprised if she routinely corners your big, friendly dog.

The Scorpio Cat, well suited to living with a fast-paced bachelor, often prefers men to women because, male or female, Scorpio Cat identifies far more strongly with the male. Let her roam the neighborhood freely (as if you really have a choice!), talk to her kindly but with a definite air of command, and buy her a collar – preferably a sturdy black one with metal studs. You can decorate it with the recommended stones.

Scorpio Cat is fiercely independent and willful. She will not fulfill your dream of lounging by the fire with your cat nestled snugly in your lap! If instead you prefer a cat who will ignore you while she concentrates on hunting down and killing a real (or imaginary) foe, congratulations.

You don't exactly cuddle up with a Scorpio Cat – unless it suits her. When she does offer to let you spread love on her, she won't be content with plain old petting. That's for sissies! Scorpio wants – and expects – you to use your imagination. Come up with surprises and fun new games when the two of you play.

Scorpio Cat will insist that you serve her meals on time. She'll also stand guard over her food bowl, warning other pets she has no intention of sharing! Born under the planet Mars, Scorpio Cat is a Water Sign, so it's not surprising that she likes her food moist. She'll want you to pamper her with soft, smooth seafood, so be prepared to buy truckloads of shrimp or lobster flavored cat food. If she arrives in your life as a stray, Scorpio meows loudly until you let her in, and then eats to her heart's content – further evidence that she knows exactly what she wants and doesn't settle for anything less.

Compatibility with other signs:

Harmony: Pisces, Cancer
Friendship: Capricorn, Virgo
Conflict: Aquarius, Taurus, Leo
Health Tips: Although she is sturdy, Scorpio Cat may experience problems with upper respiratory tract infections.
What does Scorpio Cat bring you? Scorpio Cat usually arrives during a time of radical transformation. If you succeed in establishing a rapport with your Scorpio she will pour out her tenderness and compassion on you. Scorpio Cat may also appear during a time of emotional helplessness or vulnerability. She will silently support you and channel protection. Highly intuitive, Scorpio Cat feels her loved ones' moods. She can use this ability to subconsciously protect you against any evil influence.

Sagittarius Cat

November 23-December 21

Symbol: The Centaur with the bow and arrow. Like the arrow in the Centaur's bow, Sagittarius Cat has far-reaching, free-ranging, restless, idealistic aims.
Key Words: Liberty, Independence, Adventure

Dominant Principle: "I see"
Ruling Planet: Jupiter
Stones: Topaz, Amethyst, Sapphire, Agate, Turquoise, Carbuncle, Emerald
Metals: Zinc, Tin (plate)
Lucky Day: Thursday
Unlucky Day: Wednesday

Sagittarian cat is *friendly*, *people-loving and curious*

Sagittarius Cat has a tremendous need to wander. If you keep him cooped up indoors he'll feel imprisoned – and he'll probably tell you so with long, disappointed meows. Friendly, people-loving and curious, your feline Sagittarius is a natural explorer. He is happy to be let out in the morning when you leave, and not to return until he hears your worried call at night.

What's he been doing all day? Well, first he visited that nice old lady across the street and charmed her out of another saucer of cream. Then he played tag with the children next door. Next he decided to follow the scent of another neighborhood cat to the other end of the block. His strenuous day exhausts him, but don't worry; he still has plenty of time for you, because his loyal and loving nature makes him generous to a fault. The perfect pet for children, Sagittarius Cat is always available for play. He

poses patiently for pictures, purrs when you adorn him with big red bows, and even lets you dress him up for Halloween.

Sagittarius's appetite for adventure is endless, and so is his appetite for food. (As a Fire Sign, he needs lots of fuel.) He especially loves adventurously flavored cat food, such as venison or duck. Although he has no problem sharing his food with other cats, Sagittarius eats so quickly there is simply no time for the others – blink and his dinner is gone! Feed him individually or your other feline friends will probably starve. If you go on vacation, ask a neighbor to take your Sagittarius Cat. They're probably friends already!

Compatibility with other signs:

Harmony: Aries, Leo
Friendship: Aquarius, Libra
Conflict: Pisces, Gemini, Virgo
Health Tips: Sagittarius Cat recovers very quickly from illness. Watch for problems with his lungs. Don't let him eat too much and make sure he gets lots of exercise because Sagittarian kitties can get obese, resulting in problems with diabetes.
What does Sagittarius Cat bring you? When Sagittarius Cat arrives in your life, it is a sure sign that you are going to move on. Maybe it's an exciting new job, maybe it's a foreign travel, maybe it's your outlook on life – but you're going into something new. Don't forget to take Sagittarius Cat with you! He will make an excellent travel companion. The appearance of Sagittarius Cat might also indicate a period of spiritual rebirth in your life or a new interest in metaphysical studies. In this case your cat will be your protective talisman.

Capricorn Cat

December 22-January 20

Symbol: The Goat. Capricorn is identified with various mythical "culture gods" who came from the sea (symbol of the unconscious), imparted civilization to humans, and sank back into the depths after nightfall.

Key Words: Duty, Aspiration, Ambition

Dominant Principle: "I use"

Ruling Planets: Saturn, Mars

Stones: Ruby, Onyx, Moonstone, Lazurite, Garnet

Metal: Lead

Lucky Days: Tuesday, Saturday

Unlucky Days: Monday, Thursday

Your Capricorn cat is a *born survivor*

Capricorn Cat is a cool, self-reliant creature. He doesn't seem to need anybody! Sure, it would be nice if you fixed him a comfy bed of his own, but hey, anywhere will do. Sleeping on the kitchen floor tonight because someone shut him in there by mistake? Most cats would meow pitifully, but for Capricorn – no problem.

Capricorn Cat is willing to tough out almost anything. His ruling planet is Saturn, which means he has incredible powers of endurance. Your feline Capricorn is a born survivor. Even when he's the runt of the litter, his strong survival instincts will see to it that none of the other kittens nuzzle him out of the way. He may be small, but his determination makes him a winner every time.

The perfect pet for a couple on the fast-track and without much time to spend at home, Capricorn Cat insists on patrolling his territory outside. He tends to ignore other pets in the neighborhood and refuse food from strangers, no matter how long it's been since he's eaten. Capricorn's survival instincts are so strong that, if he really gets hungry on the road, he'll dig through a garbage can or two. Get a cat door installed for your Capricorn – you'll be doing him a huge favor. With his own door, he can come in and out when he likes. You won't find your Capricorn Cat a fussy eater or even a demanding one, but you'll do well to give him simple, though substantial, foods like beef and chicken.

Although Capricorn Cat seems unblinkingly detached, don't be fooled. He needs love as much as the next kitty, but he'd rather you temper your emotion by being affectionate in a sensible way. Do not scoop him up and crush him to your bosom in a whirlwind of excitement and kitty-crazed romance. Instead, approach him calmly, respectfully, offering solid caresses for his kitty backbone. Your Capricorn Cat probably won't get too attached to any other pets you have, but if you raise him from a kitten, keep the sibling to whom he seems most attached. Despite his self-contained air Capricorn loves to feel like he belongs, and having a kitty bro to watch over will make him feel secure and safe.

Compatibility with other signs:

Harmony: Taurus, Virgo
Friendship: Pisces, Scorpio
Conflict: Aries, Cancer, Libra
Health Tips: Capricorn can suffer from thyroid disease and may even have allergic skin conditions. Even though he likes being an outdoor cat, keep him in when it's cold!
What does Capricorn Cat bring you? Capricorn Cat may come to you at the time of your greatest achievement, or his appearance may indicate a forthcoming success. His presence brings you recognition for your efforts and the culmination of an arduous phase. In any case, be ready to welcome him.

How to Choose the Best Name for Your Cat.... Without Asking the Cat!

Every name corresponds to a particular astrological number, which should be concordant with your and your pet's Zodiac signs.

To live in harmony with nature and to increase your pet's happiness and health, make sure you choose the right name for your feline companion by following the recommendations given below.

In astrology, each number corresponds to a certain planet and each planet connects to a Zodiac sign. Similarly, each letter (which becomes a vibration when pronounced) corresponds to a certain number (see table below).

1	2	3	4	5	6	7	8	9	10	11	12
A	B	C	D	E	F	G	H	I	J	K	L
M	N	O	P	Q	R	S	T	U	V	W	X
Y	Z										

Therefore, by a series of fairly simple calculations, it is possible to find the numerical value of any name. If the numerical value of a name is 10 or greater, add the digits together to find the new value of the name. Repeat this process until you get a single-digit result. For example, if you calculate a value of 49: $4+9=13$; $1+3=4$

1 Names with a numerical value of 1 are favorable for Leo and Aries. They are in disharmony with Aquarius, Cancer, and Libra. Example: BABE $=2+1+2+5=10$; $1+0=1$

2 Names with a value of 2 are favorable for Cancer or Taurus. They are in disharmony with Capricorn and Scorpio. Example: SHMUZZI $= 7+8+1+9+2+2+9 =38$; $3+8 =11$; $1+1 =2$

3 A value of 3 works well with Aries, Capricorn, and Scorpio but is in disharmony with Cancer and Libra. Example: ALICE $=1+12+9+3+5=30$; $3+0=3$

4 4 is in harmony with Gemini but does not work well with Pisces and Scorpio. Example: CLASSY $= 3+12+1+7+7+1=31$; $3+1=4$

5 5 is good for animals born under Virgo, Cancer and Pisces. It is not favorable for Sagittarius and Capricorn. Example: BARON $= 2+1+6+3+2=14$; $1+4=5$

6 6 is in harmony with Libra, Pisces and Taurus. It is in disharmony with Aries, Scorpio and Virgo. Example: BOY $=2+3+1 =6$

7 7 works well with Scorpio and Libra but is in disharmony with Aries and Cancer. Example: KISSI $= 11+9+7+7+9 =43$; $4+3 =7$

8 8 is good for Aquarius and Scorpio cats. It is not compatible with Taurus and Leo. Example: PET $= 4+5+8 =17$; $1+7 =8$.

9 9 works well for Pisces, Aquarius, and Sagittarius but is in disharmony with Leo and Gemini. DICK $= 4+9+3+11 =27$; $2+7 =9$

The following table will help you find your pet's favorable astrological number:

	In harmony (Favorable number)	In disharmony (Unfavorable number)
Aries	1, 3	6, 7
Taurus	2, 6	8
Gemini	4	9
Cancer	2, 5	1, 3, 7
Leo	1	8, 9
Virgo	5	6
Libra	6, 7	1, 3
Scorpio	3, 7, 8	2, 4, 6
Sagittarius	9	5
Capricorn	3	2, 5
Aquarius	8, 9	1
Pisces	5, 6, 9	4

Finding the Best Time to Let Your Cat Out.... Without Asking Him!

The best times to let your cat outside are the hours ruled by Mercury and Moon. Each day of the week is ruled by one planet:

Sunday	–	Sun
Monday	–	Moon
Tuesday	–	Mars
Wednesday	–	Mercury
Thursday	–	Jupiter
Friday	–	Venus
Saturday	–	Saturn

The planets also rule the hours of every day. The first hour following sunrise is ruled by the day's ruling planet. Therefore, on Sunday, the first hour belongs to the Sun; on Monday, to the Moon; on Tuesday, to Mars; on Wednesday, to

Mercury; and so on. The planets rule each subsequent hour in a rotating sequence, re-beginning every eighth hour with the day's ruling planet. (See the table below.)

For example: On Sunday, the sequence begins with the Sun and continues with Venus, Mercury, Moon, Saturn, Jupiter, Mars, Sun, and so on. On Tuesday, while the pattern remains the same, the sequence begins with Mars – Tuesday's ruling planet – followed by Sun, Venus, Mercury, Moon, Saturn, Jupiter, Mars, Sun, etc.

After sunset, the planet sequence begins with the fifth planet after the day's ruling planet. Then the same rotating sequence applies. For instance: On Sunday, the first hour after sunset will be Jupiter; the second – Mars; the third – Sun; and so on. (See table below.) If your count goes past midnight, it should be considered the next day and thus ignored. Remember: The best hours to walk your pet are those ruled by Mercury and the Moon.

(After Sunrise)

	1st hour	2nd hour	3rd hour	4th hour	5th hour	6th hour	7th hour	8th hou
SUNDAY	SUN	VENUS	MERCURY	MOON	SATURN	JUPITER	MARS	SUN
MONDAY	MOON	SATURN	JUPITER	MARS	SUN	VENUS	MERCURY	MOON
TUESDAY	MARS	SUN	VENUS	MERCURY	MOON	SATURN	JUPITER	MARS
WEDNESDAY	MERCURY	MOON	SATURN	JUPITER	MARS	SUN	VENUS	MERC
THURSDAY	JUPITER	MARS	SUN	VENUS	MERCURY	MOON	SATURN	JUPITE
FRIDAY	VENUS	MERCURY	MOON	SATURN	JUPITER	MARS	SUN	VENU
SATURDAY	SATURN	JUPITER	MARS	SUN	VENUS	MERCURY	MOON	SATUF

(After Sunset)

	1st hour	2nd hour	3rd hour	4th hour	5th hour	6th hour	7th hour
SUNDAY	JUPITER	MARS	SUN	VENUS	MERCURY	MOON	SATURN
MONDAY	VENUS	MERCURY	MOON	SATURN	JUPITER	MARS	SUN
TUESDAY	SATURN	JUPITER	MARS	SUN	VENUS	MERCURY	MOON
WEDNESDAY	SUN	VENUS	MERCURY	MOON	SATURN	JUPITER	MARS
THURSDAY	MOON	SATURN	JUPITER	MARS	SUN	VENUS	MERCURY
FRIDAY	MARS	SUN	VENUS	MERCURY	MOON	SATURN	JUPITER
SATURDAY	MERCURY	MOON	SATURN	JUPITER	MARS	SUN	VENUS

Use these tables to quickly find the hours ruled by Mercury and Moon.

After Sunrise:		After Sunset:	
Sunday	3, 4 and 10,11	Sunday	5, 6 and 12,13
Monday	1 and 7,8	Monday	2, 3 and 9,10
Tuesday	4, 5 and 11,12	Tuesday	6, 7 and 13,14
Wednesday	1, 2 and 8,9	Wednesday	3, 4 and 10,11
Thursday	5, 6 and 12,13	Thursday	1, 7 and 8
Friday	2, 3 and 9,10	Friday	4, 5 and 11,12
Saturday	6, 7 and 13,14	Saturday	1, 2 and 8,9

Cat's Astrological
Birth Certificate

©Aquarius Cat

Aquarius Cat
January 21-February 19

Symbol: The Water Carrier. Aquarius – an Air Sign – belongs to the element which links all living beings: the life force that flows from the atmosphere through our bodies, and out into the atmosphere again.
Key words: Friendship, Eccentricity, Freedom
Dominant principle: "I know" **Ruling Planet:** Saturn
Stones: Light Sapphire, Opal, Amethyst, Garnet **Metal:** Tin **Lucky Days:** Wednesday, Saturday

What does Aquarius Cat bring you? From the moment he appears in your house, Aquarius Cat compensates for any lack of friendship and security in your life.. He may become a very loyal friend, accompanying you on trips like a devoted dog. He could even protect you against attacks. If Aquarius Cat has found you when the sun is in Aquarius, he is almost certainly a gift from someone in the spirit world. In giving you this special cat, the sender is telling you that you are loved, missed, and remembered.

Your
Cat's
Photo
Here

Cat's Name_____

Cat's Nickname_____

Cat's Date of Birth_____

KoZmoPets

Cat's Astrological
Birth Certificate

Pisces Cat
February 20-March 20

©Pisces Cat

Symbol: Two fish joined together but pulling in opposite directions, embodying Pisces' dual and vacillating nature.

Key words: : Sensitive, Indecisive, Compassionate.

Dominant principle: "I believe" **Ruling Planet:** Jupiter

Stones: Sapphire, Moonstone **Metal:** Zinc **Lucky Days:** Monday, Thursday, Friday

What does Pisces Cat bring you? If you get a Pisces Cat (or any cat during the Pisces period) it indicates Karmic ties. You have been destined to meet! She came to share your solitary existence and heal your wounds with her love.

Your
Cat's
Photo
Here

Cat's Name_____

Cat's Nickname_____

Cat's Date of Birth_____

KoZmoPets

Cat's Astrological
Birth Certificate

©Aries Cat

Aries Cat
March 21-April 20

Symbol: The Ram. Aries cat is an aggressive leader, always ready to accept a challenge
Key words: Enthusiasm, Pluck, Aggression
Dominant principle: "I am" **Ruling Planets:** Mars, Sun
Stones: Diamond, Ruby, Amethyst **Metals:** Iron, Steel **Lucky Days:** Tuesday, Sunday

What does Aries Cat bring you? Aries Cat marks a new cycle in your life. Her arrival signals a time of change and new beginnings.

Your
Cat's
Photo
Here

Cat's Name_____

Cat's Nickname_____

Cat's Date of Birth_____

KoZmoPets

Cat's Astrological
Birth Certificate

©Taurus Cat

Taurus Cat
April 21-May 21

Symbol: The Bull. Like his symbol – a powerfully built, possessive animal – Taurus is unflinching in attack
Key words: Practicality, Possessiveness, Hedonism
Dominant principle: "I have" **Ruling Planets:** Venus, Moon
Stones: Sapphire, Agate, Turquoise, Nephrite **Metal:** Copper **Lucky Days:** Monday, Friday

What does Taurus Cat bring you? This cat possesses a golden paw. When he comes into your life,
financial improvements are just around the corner; if you are in a difficult phase of your life,
Taurus Cat will prove a huge emotional support.

Your
Cat's
Photo
Here

Cat's Name_____

Cat's Nickname_____

Cat's Date of Birth_____

KoZmoPets

Cat's Astrological
Birth Certificate

©Gemini Cat

Gemini Cat
May 22-June 21

Symbol: The Twins. Gemini's dual nature is reflected in its symbol, which resembles the Roman Numeral II. Gemini Cat may display two very distinct personalities.

Key words: Inventive, Studious, Active, Sly

Dominant principle: "I think" **Ruling Planet:** Mercury

Stones: Agate, Crystal, Garnet **Metals:** Gold, Silver **Lucky Days:** Wednesday, Sunday

What does Gemini Cat bring you? Gemini's greatest gift is protection.
She always senses – and warns you – of approaching trouble.

Your
Cat's
Photo
Here

Cat's Name_____

Cat's Nickname_____

Cat's Date of Birth_____

KoZmoPets

Cat's Astrological
Birth Certificate

©Cancer Cat

Cancer Cat
June 22-July 23

Symbol: The Crab. Like the sea creature that represents him, Cancer Cat has a soft, sensitive interior and a protective exterior shell.

Key words: Domestic, Security, Emotional, Support

Dominant principle: "I feel" **Ruling Planet:** Moon

Stones: Moonstone, Ruby, Emerald **Metal:** Silver **Lucky Days:** Monday, Thursday

What does Cancer Cat bring you? Cancer Cat offers you two great gifts: security and protection.

Your
Cat's
Photo
Here

Cat's Name_____

Cat's Nickname_____

Cat's Date of Birth_____

KoZmoPets

Cat's Astrological
Birth Certificate

©Leo Cat

Leo Cat
July 24-August 23

Symbol: The Lion. Leo Cat, with his power, his roar, and his regal attitude, takes his cues from the King of the Beasts.
Key words: Power, Generosity, Charisma
Dominant principle: "I will" **Ruling Planet:** Sun
Stones: Amber, Topaz, Emerald, Ruby, Onyx **Metal:** Gold **Lucky Day:** Sunday

What does Leo Cat bring you? Leo Cat's presence reminds you to have confidence in yourself. Walk upright, with your head high, especially when the world has been giving you a hard time.

Your Cat's Photo Here	Cat's Name_____ Cat's Nickname_____ Cat's Date of Birth_____

KoZmoPets

Cat's Astrological
Birth Certificate

©Virgo Cat

Virgo Cat
August 24-September 23

Symbol: The Virgin. The only feminine figure in the Zodiac, the Virgin holds an ear of wheat, which symbolizes fertility. She was worshiped as the Earth goddess throughout the ancient world.

Key words: Service, Practicality, Loyalty

Dominant principle: "I analyze" **Ruling Planet:** Mercury

Stones: Agate, Malachite, Carnelian, Topaz, Nephrite, and Yellow Sapphire

Metals: Copper, Tin **Lucky Day:** Wednesday

What does Virgo Cat bring you? Compassionate and loving to the max.
Virgo Cat offers oodles and oodles of relief to anyone in discomfort.

Your
Cat's
Photo
Here

Cat's Name_____

Cat's Nickname_____

Cat's Date of Birth_____

KoZmoPets

Cat's Astrological
Birth Certificate

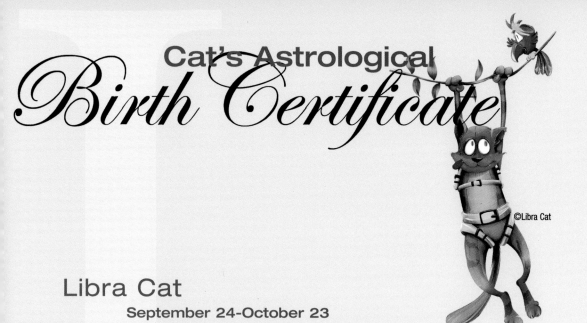

©Libra Cat

Libra Cat
September 24-October 23

Symbol: The Scales. Libra's symbol is the only inanimate object among the Zodiac signs. Libras seek in others the balancing qualities they lack in themselves. This results in their frequent indecisiveness.

Key words: Cooperation, Companionship, Balance

Dominant principle: "I balance" **Ruling Planet:** Venus

Stones: Opal, Lazurite, Pearl, Chrysolite, and Diamond **Lucky Days:** Friday, Saturday

What does Libra Cat bring you? Because Libra Cat often supplies the emotional support we lack in our human relationships, this cat may arrive in your house when those relationships are suffering. Libra can restore broken harmony in the family and even at work. Try sharing pictures of your kitty companion with coworkers. He may provide the common ground you need to get back on the right track.

If you appreciate his dedication, Libra is a very loyal friend.

Your
Cat's
Photo
Here

Cat's Name_____

Cat's Nickname_____

Cat's Date of Birth_____

Cat's Astrological
Birth Certificate

©Scorpio Cat

Scorpio Cat
October 24–November 22

Symbol: The Scorpion and the Eagle. Together they rise above temptation.
This sign is associated with both the life force and the life cycle.
Key words: Tenacity, Rebirth, Mystery
Dominant principle: "I desire" **Ruling Planets:** Pluto, Mars
Stones: Ruby, Topaz, Aquamarine, Coral, and Malachite **Metals:** Iron, Steel **Lucky Day:** Tuesday

What does Scorpio Cat bring you? Scorpio Cat usually arrives during a time of radical transformation. If you succeed in establishing a rapport with your Scorpio Cat she will pour out her tenderness and compassion on you. Scorpio Cat may also appear during a time of emotional helplessness or vulnerability. She will silently support you and channel protection. Highly intuitive, Scorpio Cat feels her loved ones' moods. She can use this ability to subconsciously protect you against any evil influence.

Your
Cat's
Photo
Here

Cat's Name_____

Cat's Nickname_____

Cat's Date of Birth_____

KoZmoPets

Cat's Astrological
Birth Certificate

©Sagittarius Cat

Sagittarius Cat
November 23–December 21

Symbol: The Centaur with the bow and arrow. Like the arrow in the Centaur's bow, Sagittarius Cat has far-reaching, free-ranging, restless, and idealistic aims.
Key words: Liberty, Independence, Adventure **Dominant principle:** "I see"
Ruling Planet: Jupiter **Stones:** Topaz, Amethyst, Sapphire, Agate, Turquoise, Carbuncle, Emerald
Metals: Zinc, Tin (plate) **Lucky Day:** Thursday

What does Sagittarius Cat bring you? When Sagittarius Cat arrives in your life, it is a sure sign that you are going to move on. Maybe it's an exciting new job, maybe it's a foreign travel, maybe it's your outlook on life – but you're going into something new. Don't forget to take Sagittarius Cat with you! He will make an excellent travel companion. The appearance of Sagittarius Cat might also indicate a period of spiritual rebirth in your life or a new interest in metaphysical studies. In this case your cat will be your protective talisman.

Your
Cat's
Photo
Here

Cat's Name_____

Cat's Nickname_____

Cat's Date of Birth_____

KoZmoPets

Cat's Astrological
Birth Certificate

©Capricorn Cat

Capricorn Cat
December 22–January 20

Symbol: The Goat. Capricorn is identified with various mythical "culture gods" who came from the sea (symbol of the unconscious), imparted civilization to humans, and sank back into the depths after nightfall.

Key words: Duty, Aspiration, Ambition

Dominant principle: "I use" **Ruling Planets:** Saturn, Mars

Stones: Ruby, Onyx, Moonstone, Lazurite, Garnet **Metal:** Lead **Lucky Days:** Tuesday, Saturday

What does Capricorn Cat bring you? Capricorn Cat may come to you at the time of your greatest achievement, or his appearance may indicate a forthcoming success. His presence brings you recognition for your efforts and the culmination of an arduous phase. In any case, be ready to welcome him.

Your
Cat's
Photo
Here

Cat's Name_____

Cat's Nickname_____

Cat's Date of Birth_____

KoZmoPets

Notes

Notes

_____

_____

_____

_____

_____

_____

_____

_____

_____

_____

Notes

Notes

Notes

_____

_____

_____

_____

_____

_____

_____

_____

_____

Notes

Notes

Notes

Notes

_____

_____

_____

_____

_____

_____

_____

_____

_____

_____

Notes

Notes

Notes

About the Author

Luba Matusovsky, a noted author/journalist/artist/art collector/inventor and – not least – pet lover, wrote Your Cat's Lifetime Horoscope because she wanted in an entertaining, informative way to help pet lovers better understand their pets and the role they play in each other's life.

A native of Moscow, Luba came to America from Russia to fulfill a promise to her father, and now lives in Denver with her husband, Edward. Other members of her family live in California.

She has many friends all over the world. She loves to travel and is a good cook. The founder of Pets Horoscopes, LLC, Luba is also the author of Your Dog's Lifetime Horoscope as a part of "KozmoPets" series line of greeting cards, posters, calendars, etc., portraying the same loveable, charming astro cats and dogs images found within her books.

Mrs. Matusovsky has a degree in economics, worked as a project coordinator at different international exhibitions and as a journalist for newspapers and magazines. She continues to pursue her interests in inventions (has a US patent for a household device), astrology, history, classical and jazz music. Your Cat's Lifetime Horoscope is Mrs. Matusovsky's first book to be published in the USA.

Your Cat's Lifetime Horoscope
By Luba Matusovsky
2nd edition
Cover and book design: Vladimir Sonkin
Illustrator: Oleg Urlov
Editor: Ron Kenner
ISBN-10: 0-98268-340-5
ISBN-13: 978-0-9826834-0-8
$17.95 (CAN $19.95)
Pets Horoscopes, LLC (2010)

Published in 2010 by Pets Horoscopes, LLC
www.kozmopets.com
Printed in China